Crunchy Parenting

A Natural Parenting Guide That'll Teach You Everything You'll Ever Need to Know About Babywearing, Bodily Autonomy, Breastfeeding, Cloth Diapering, and More!

Madi Haire & HowExpert Press

Copyright www.HowExpert.com

Recommended Resources

www.HowExpert.com – Short 'how to' guides on unique topics by everyday experts!

www.HowExpert.com/parenting - Additional resource for parents.

COPYRIGHT, LEGAL NOTICE AND DISCLAIMER:

COPYRIGHT © BY HOWEXPERT.COM – OWNED BY HOT METHODS, INC. ALL RIGHTS RESERVED WORLDWIDE. NO PART OF THIS PUBLICATION MAY BE REPRODUCED IN ANY FORM OR BY ANY MEANS, INCLUDING SCANNING, PHOTOCOPYING, OR OTHERWISE WITHOUT PRIOR WRITTEN PERMISSION OF THE COPYRIGHT HOLDER.

DISCLAIMER AND TERMS OF USE: PLEASE NOTE THAT MUCH OF THIS PUBLICATION IS BASED ON PERSONAL EXPERIENCE AND ANECDOTAL EVIDENCE. ALTHOUGH THE AUTHOR AND PUBLISHER HAVE MADE EVERY REASONABLE ATTEMPT TO ACHIEVE COMPLETE ACCURACY OF THE CONTENT IN THIS GUIDE, THEY ASSUME NO RESPONSIBILITY FOR ERRORS OR OMISSIONS. ALSO, YOU SHOULD USE THIS INFORMATION AS YOU SEE FIT, AND AT YOUR OWN RISK. YOUR PARTICULAR SITUATION MAY NOT BE EXACTLY SUITED TO THE EXAMPLES ILLUSTRATED HERE; IN FACT, IT'S LIKELY THAT THEY WON'T BE THE SAME, AND YOU SHOULD ADJUST YOUR USE OF THE INFORMATION AND RECOMMENDATIONS ACCORDINGLY.

THE AUTHOR AND PUBLISHER DO NOT WARRANT THE PERFORMANCE, EFFECTIVENESS OR APPLICABILITY OF ANY SITES LISTED OR LINKED TO IN THIS BOOK. ALL LINKS ARE FOR INFORMATION PURPOSES ONLY AND ARE NOT WARRANTED FOR CONTENT, ACCURACY OR ANY OTHER IMPLIED OR EXPLICIT PURPOSE.

ANY TRADEMARKS, SERVICE MARKS, PRODUCT NAMES OR NAMED FEATURES ARE ASSUMED TO BE THE PROPERTY OF THEIR RESPECTIVE OWNERS, AND ARE USED ONLY FOR REFERENCE. THERE IS NO IMPLIED ENDORSEMENT IF WE USE ONE OF THESE TERMS.

NO PART OF THIS BOOK MAY BE REPRODUCED, STORED IN A RETRIEVAL SYSTEM, OR TRANSMITTED BY ANY OTHER MEANS: ELECTRONIC, MECHANICAL, PHOTOCOPYING, RECORDING, OR OTHERWISE, WITHOUT THE PRIOR WRITTEN PERMISSION OF THE AUTHOR.

ANY VIOLATION BY STEALING THIS BOOK OR DOWNLOADING OR SHARING IT ILLEGALLY WILL BE PROSECUTED BY LAWYERS TO THE FULLEST EXTENT. THIS PUBLICATION IS PROTECTED UNDER THE US COPYRIGHT ACT OF 1976 AND ALL OTHER APPLICABLE INTERNATIONAL, FEDERAL, STATE AND LOCAL LAWS AND ALL RIGHTS ARE RESERVED, INCLUDING RESALE RIGHTS: YOU ARE NOT ALLOWED TO GIVE OR SELL THIS GUIDE TO ANYONE ELSE.

THIS PUBLICATION IS DESIGNED TO PROVIDE ACCURATE AND AUTHORITATIVE INFORMATION WITH REGARD TO THE SUBJECT MATTER COVERED. IT IS SOLD WITH THE UNDERSTANDING THAT THE AUTHORS AND PUBLISHERS ARE NOT ENGAGED IN RENDERING LEGAL, FINANCIAL, OR OTHER PROFESSIONAL ADVICE. LAWS AND PRACTICES OFTEN VARY FROM STATE TO STATE AND IF LEGAL OR OTHER EXPERT ASSISTANCE IS REQUIRED, THE SERVICES OF A PROFESSIONAL SHOULD BE SOUGHT. THE AUTHORS AND PUBLISHER SPECIFICALLY DISCLAIM ANY LIABILITY THAT IS INCURRED FROM THE USE OR APPLICATION OF THE CONTENTS OF THIS BOOK.

VISIT OUR WEBSITE AT WWW.HOWEXPERT.COM
COPYRIGHT BY HOT METHODS, INC. ALL RIGHTS RESERVED WORLDWIDE.

Table of Contents

Recommended Resources 2
Introduction: Crunchy Parenting is a More Natural Approach to Raising Kids... 9
Chapter 1: Crunchy Birthing 10
   Education and Preparation for a Crunchy Natural Birth 10
   How to Manage Natural Labor as a Crunchy Mom 12
      Relax... 12
      Doulas and Other Support People 14
   Crunchy Birth Planning...15
   First Crunchy Hours with Baby............................... 17
      Delayed Cord Clamping 17
      Skin to Skin Contact..18
      Limit Stimulation..19
Chapter 2: Breastfeeding: Feeding Your Baby the Crunchy Way 20
   Benefits of Breastfeeding That Crunchy Parents Understand 21
      Breastmilk Changes 22
      Breastfed Babies Don't Get Sick as Often 23
      Breastmilk is Free 24
      Benefits of Breastfeeding for the Mother 25
      Other Benefits of Breastfeeding.......................... 25
   Getting Off to a Good Start with Breastfeeding as a Crunchy Family..27
      Educate Yourself 27
      Start as Soon as Possible..................................... 28
      Nurse on Demand 28
      Surround Yourself with Support......................... 30
      Seek Help When You Need It 30
   Potential Problems and How Crunchy Moms Combat Them 31
      Poor Latch 32
      Engorgement, Clogged Ducts, and Mastitis 34

Crunchy Families Practice Full-Term Breastfeeding 36
Crunchy Alternative Uses of Breastmilk 37
   Healing Uses of Breastmilk............................... 38
   Milk Baths 39
   Cooking with Breastmilk................................... 40
   Breastmilk Products..41
Chapter 3: Crunchy Diet.. 42
   Crunchy Families Practice Baby-Led Weaning..... 43
   Making Your Own Baby Food as a Crunchy Parent 45
   Eating Organic is Essential with a Crunchy Lifestyle 46
      Organic Food is Safer... 46
      Organic Food is Healthier................................. 46
      Organic Food is More Environmentally Friendly 47
Chapter 4: How Crunchy Parents Diaper Their Babies 48
   Benefits That Crunchy Parents Get from Cloth Diapering 49
      Cloth Diapers Are Better for the Environment . 49
      Cloth Diapers Save Money................................ 50
      Cloth Diapers Are Safer for Your Baby.............. 50
      Cloth Diapers Are Cuter..................................... 50
   Types of Cloth Diapers for Crunchy Parents to Choose From 51
      Flats and Prefolds 51
      Contours and Fitteds.. 52
      Pocket Diapers 52
      Hybrid Fitteds 53
      All-in-Ones and All-in-Twos..............................53
      Cloth Diaper Covers 54
   Crunchy Parents Need to Know How to Care for Cloth Diapers 54
      Storing Used Diapers Until Wash Day 55

- Washing Diapers 57
- Drying Diapers 57

Chapter 5: Babywearing is a Hallmark of Crunchy Parenting 59

- Benefits of Babywearing that Crunchy Parents Get 59
  - Worn Babies Cry Less 60
  - Babywearing Frees Your Hands 61
  - Babywearing is Convenient............................... 61
  - Babywearing Helps to Keep Your Baby Safe 62
- Types of Baby Carriers for Crunchy Parents to Choose From 63
  - Pouch Slings 64
  - Ring Slings 64
  - Stretchy Wraps 65
  - Soft Structured Carriers (SSCs) 65
  - Mei Tais 66
  - Woven Wraps 66
- Babywearing Safety is a Must When Parenting Crunchy..67
  - Tight 67
  - In Sight 67
  - Close Enough to Kiss.. 68
  - Keep Chin Off Chest... 68
  - Supported Back 68
  - Babywearing Safety in High or Low Temperatures 69
- Basic Carries in a Woven Wrap for Crunchy Parents to Learn 70
  - Front Wrap Cross Carry.................................... 71
  - Rucksack Carry 75

Chapter 6: Co-Sleeping: Why Crunchy Parents Sleep Better 80

- Benefits Crunchy Parents Get from Co-Sleeping ...81
  - Co-Sleeping Babies Wake Less Often 81
  - Co-Sleeping Gives You Peace of Mind 82

    Co-Sleeping Increases Bond and Attachment ... 82
Co-Sleeping Safety That Crunchy Parents Need to Know 83
    No Smoking, Drinking, or Drugs 83
    Sleep on a Safe Surface 84
    Bed Sharing is Safest When Baby is Breastfed .. 85
Crunchy Parents Know to Ignore the Myths of Co-Sleeping 87
    "Bed Sharing is Dangerous" 87
    "Your Baby Will Never Sleep on Their Own" 87
    "You're Preventing Your Child from Learning Independence" 88

Chapter 7: Crunchy Parents Believe in Bodily Autonomy 89
Their Body, Their Choice 89
Drawbacks of Circumcision that Crunchy Parents Avoid 91
    Circumcision Causes Trauma 93
    Circumcision Carries Serious Risks 94
    Circumcision Causes the Loss of Important Functions 95
Cognitive Dissonance 96
Proper Intact Care for Crunchy Parents and Their Sons 96

Chapter 8: Crunchy Parents Choose Natural Immunity 98
Crunchy Parents Understand the Dangers of Vaccinating 98
Problems with the Pro-Vax Argument 100
    Herd Immunity is a Lie 100
    Unvaccinated Children Do Not Pose a Risk 101
    You Are Not Putting Your Child in Danger by Not Vaccinating 102
Crunchier Ways to Boost Immunity 103
    Breastfeeding 103
    Diet 104

Environmental Factors 104
Conclusion: Crunchy Parenting is Natural and Easy
....105
About the Expert 106
Recommended Resources 107

Introduction: Crunchy Parenting is a More Natural Approach to Raising Kids

Crunchy parenting, and even crunchy living in general can have many different definitions. Some people think that crunchy and hippie are practically synonyms, but that isn't necessarily true. Really, crunchy parenting is generally all about making more natural choices in the way that you live and raise your children. The main thing that I have found that most crunchy parents and families have in common is being very open-minded and having a desire to seek out information.

This open-mindedness combined with a desire to learn is what tends to lead parents to these similar, more natural choices. Crunchy families don't simply accept that things are just the way they are. They research, seek out information for themselves, and then make their decisions based off of fact and evidence rather than off of what they have been told by others. Many are surprised to find that once you start digging, you will find that the things that are accepted as normal in our society are often not the best choices.

Chapter 1: Crunchy Birthing

Crunchy birthing typically means going through labor and giving birth to your baby naturally without any interventions or pain medications. Of course, there are times when interventions are necessary and lifesaving, but in most cases, they are unneeded. The majority of the time, if a pregnant mother is educated, prepared, and supported, she can achieve a natural, normal birth with no complications or the need of any interventions. Ironically, birth interventions often cause problems that lead to further intervention. It's a cycle that has a lot to do with the ridiculously high rate of cesareans that are now happening.

While I, thankfully, avoided a cesarean, I do have some first-hand experience with this cycle of intervention. With my first pregnancy with my son, I was diagnosed with preeclampsia and therefore my doctor insisted on induction. The Pitocin that I received had many negative effects, including dropping my son's heartrate multiple times, and ended up with me getting an episiotomy among other undesirable events. Everything about my daughter's birth, however, ended up perfect with zero interventions.

Education and Preparation for a Crunchy Natural Birth

Your crunchy parenting journey can start from the very beginning when you first discover that you're expecting a precious new addition to your family. Spending your pregnancy making healthy and generally more natural choices will help you prepare for your crunchy birth experience and caring for your new little one.

In modern day society, the natural experience of labor and birthing is now viewed in the medical world as if it's an illness that must be treated rather than a miraculous natural process to be observed with assistance ready on the rare occasions that it's actually necessary. I remember many people acting like I was insane because I planned to birth without pain medication. Some of them laughed as if I would never actually accomplish my natural births, which only made me more determined than ever.

One of the most important things you can do to help ensure that you achieve the natural birth that most crunchy moms aim for is to prepare and educate yourself. There are many different classes and programs that you can go through that will help you learn about the natural process of birth as well as teach you ways to naturally cope with labor.

Additionally, it's a great idea to take steps to educate yourself through your own research about the natural process of labor and how your body does what it does. Learning about exactly what your body is doing can help you to more easily get through the process naturally.

In addition to taking classes, I spent all of my first pregnancy constantly researching everything I could that had anything to do with pregnancy, labor, birth, and newborn care so that I would be as prepared as possible for anything and everything that I was to encounter. I wanted to be absolutely sure that all of my choices were well-informed and evidence-based.

How to Manage Natural Labor as a Crunchy Mom

In our society, women are taught from the time that they are little girls that labor and birth is a horrific experience that will be the most painful thing that they ever endure. It is engrained in our minds to believe that birth is scary, painful, and that it can't be done without pain medication. However, the truth is that birth is a completely natural and normal human experience that doesn't have to be any of those things. A huge part of achieving a natural birth is simply understanding the process of labor and birth as well as having a good mind set.

Relax

Your preconceived notions have a lot to do with your experience. Knowing what to expect and how your body works will help to ease your fears which plays a big role in easing the discomfort of labor. This is because of something known as the fear-tension-pain cycle. Basically, when you expect and fear being in a great deal of pain, your body becomes very tense. That tension that you hold throughout your body fights the natural process of your uterus contacting to open up your cervix.

Your uterus is made up of multiple layers of muscles. The outermost layer of muscle is made up of long muscle fibers that run up and down the outside of your uterus concentrated at the top of your uterus. The innermost layer of muscle is made up of circular muscles that run around your uterus horizontally and are concentrated towards the bottom of your uterus. These layers work together during labor.

When you experience a contraction during labor, the outer layer of your uterus is tightening and the muscles are pulling up towards the top of your uterus. This pulling up of the outer muscles also pulls on the inner muscles helping them to relax and thin, opening up your cervix to allow the passage of your baby through the birth canal.

When you are fearful and therefore tense during labor, you're fighting the muscles in your uterus and that not only causes pain as your body fights the process, but it also prolongs the process. If you are able to relax and trust your body to do what it's made to do, then your labor is almost guaranteed to be easier and shorter. Even with the induction process and complications that came along because of it, my labor with my son was only about 12 hours from when they started Pitocin to when he was born. My daughter's birth, which had zero interventions, was only 6 hours from the time my water broke until she was born.

In addition to relaxing and trusting yourself, there are other valuable techniques that you can use to help you get through your labor. Some women choose self-hypnosis to help them go into a state of deep relaxation during labor. Others use specialized breathing techniques and some women use visualization techniques. There are many ways to get through labor without pain medication and they all are centered around helping you to relax.

Doulas and Other Support People

One of the most vital things when it comes to achieving a natural birth is surrounding yourself with support. Ideally, you have a partner that can go through the process of preparation and education with you during your pregnancy and then be there for you throughout labor and birth. I was very blessed to have both my husband and my sister with me at both of my births. It's also very important to choose a pregnancy care provider that is on board with your plan to birth naturally and is prepared to support your decisions in regard to your labor and birth.

Midwives over obstetricians are typically friendlier to natural birth and statistics reveal that patients of midwives are much more likely to achieve their desired birth outcomes. However, with the right obstetrician, you can still certainly achieve your natural birth. The important thing is to meet with different care providers when you first find out your pregnant and find someone that you really click with and someone that will support you and your decisions.

On top of your health care provider and your partner, it can be a wonderful idea to hire a doula as well. A doula is a person that supports a woman throughout her pregnancy, labor, birth, and often for period of time after her baby arrives. Your doula, while not a medical professional, will be highly trained in childbirth and can guide you through everything and be there to answer any questions you have. They can help you advocate for yourself to health care providers, especially in a hospital setting, and will stay with you for your entire labor and birth.

Some couples worry that the doula will take the place of the partner during this very intimate time in their lives; however, the doula actually can help your partner know exactly what to do and how they can help you and be involved in the process. Your doula can also do things like run and get something out of the car while your partner remains with your or vice versa. If your partner needs to do something like go get a bite to eat, your doula will remain by your side so that you never have to be alone. If you do not have a partner, or your partner is unable to attend the birth for some reason, a doula will be of especially good use to you as you won't have to go through it all alone.

Crunchy Birth Planning

If you want to have a crunchy and natural birth experience, having a solid birth plan is a must. This is especially true if you opt for a hospital birth. A birth plan is simply a written out, or ideally typed out, plan of all of your preferences for your labor and birth. If you have a doula, they can help you write out your birth plan in an effective and clear way. They will be familiar with the types of things that you will need to write down and how to word things.

A crunchy birth plan would typically include things like how you don't want to receive pain medication for labor, how you would like your baby placed on your chest immediately after birth, how your baby shouldn't receive any artificial nipples or anything other than breastmilk, and just any other things that you prefer for your labor and birth.

The best way to have an effective birth plan is to keep it short and to the point. Don't explain your choices in the birth plan. Instead, simply write exactly what you want. For example, don't write, "I don't want my baby to have any artificial nipples because I plan on feeding my baby directly from the breast and don't want to cause any nipple confusion." Instead, write, "Do not give my baby artificial nipples." You should, however, discuss your birth plan with your pregnancy care provider sometime in early to mid-pregnancy to make sure they understand your desires and that you are both on the same page.

You'll also want to type out and print your birth plan if at all possible. This way you have something easy-to-read and professional-looking that will be more likely to be taken seriously. You should print several copies of your birth plan. Give one to your pregnancy care provider when you discuss the plan, and keep several copies in the bag that you intend to take with you to the hospital or birth center. In the case of homebirth, just keep some copies around your home.

First Crunchy Hours with Baby

When your baby first enters the world, they will be suddenly hit with many new sensations and experiences. They will be easily overwhelmed and overloaded. There are some important things that you can do to help ease this transition. There are several practices that are considered to be crunchy that you can use to get your baby off to a good – and crunchy – start.

Delayed Cord Clamping

There are some very important things you'll want to do once your little one arrives. The first thing that you'll want to consider is delayed cord clamping. In most cases, the umbilical cord, which attaches your baby to your placenta, is immediately clamped and cut once the baby is born. However, studies show that by delaying the clamping and cutting of the umbilical cord, the blood from the cord and the placenta will continue to flow into baby's body.

This gives the baby a higher blood volume than if they had their cord immediately clamped and cut. It also gives your baby many health benefits from the cord blood. You'll know when it is safe to cut the cord because the cord will stop pulsating and will go from blue in color to white in color once the baby receives all of his or her blood.

___Skin to Skin Contact___

Another important thing that should happen immediately after your baby is born is skin to skin contact between you and your baby. The transition from the womb to the world can be overwhelming and scary for your little baby and the last thing that they want is to be separated from you. Placing your naked baby on your bare chest has many health benefits and helps your little one to feel safe and secure. Your baby can wear a diaper during this time, but no clothing nor any blankets should be in-between you and your baby.

Your body has an amazing design and is the perfect and most natural "incubator" for your baby. Laying your baby skin to skin on your bare chest helps them to regulate their breathing, their body temperature, their blood pressure, and their blood sugar. It keeps them calm and soothed. It helps you to feel relaxed knowing they are happy and safe. It also facilitates a good start to breastfeeding and helps your milk supply to come in.

Once your baby emerges, they should immediately be placed on your chest. Your baby should be completely naked other than their diaper. Your chest should also be bare and your baby should lay tummy down in-between your breasts. It's also a good idea to have a blanket over top of your baby during this time to prevent the air from negatively affecting their temperature or making them uncomfortable.

Your baby should remain on your chest for at least one solid hour before anyone else holds them or they have their weight and other stats checked. You can request that these things are postponed until you are ready for them. This is the best time for you to initiate breastfeeding as well. Even once this first period of skin to skin is over, it is very beneficial to practice it regularly and often.

<u>Limit Stimulation</u>

During your baby's first hours, you should also limit stimulation. Keeping your baby on your chest should help to do this, but you should also avoid a lot of loud noises and bright lights. Keep the lights dimmed and talk softly to your baby as they will recognize your voice and find comfort in the familiar sound.

Try to keep the environment around your new baby calm and don't spend too much time passing your baby around from person to person. It's actually best to limit visitors as much as possible to help ease this difficult transition for your baby and allow your baby as well as yourself to get some much-needed rest and bonding time.

Chapter 2: Breastfeeding: Feeding Your Baby the Crunchy Way

Breastfeeding is the natural and biologically normal way to feed your baby and being a crunchy parent is all about following what is natural. There can be a stigma on breastfeeding in today's society. This is because formula became so popular for so many years that many of today's adults are unfamiliar with breastfeeding.

Today's society has oversexualized the female breast so severely that many people only see breasts in a sexual context even though they exist literally for the sole purpose of feeding babies. It is definitely true that breasts can be used in a sexual context and there is nothing wrong with that, but the same is true of hands and even feet. In fact, many people don't realize that sexual attraction to breasts is just an extremely popular fetish.

However, it becomes a serious problem when our society has no problem using breasts as a marketing tool for selling anything from food to cars, but then gets offended when seeing a mother use her breasts for their intended purpose of feeding her hungry baby. Some people go so far as to attempt to shame a breastfeeding mother as if she should feel guilty for using her body in a non-sexual way.

The good news is that tides are turning. As we learn more about breastmilk and the amazing benefits of breastfeeding, the rates of breastfeeding are steadily rising. This is good news, not only because it means healthier babies and therefore healthier adults in the future, but it is also helping to normalize breastfeeding and wipe away any stigma associated with it.

There's more good news too! Breastfeeding in public is protected by both federal law as well as state law in all 50 states. The exact laws vary in every state, but they all protect a mother's right to feed her baby wherever she needs to do so. It is illegal for anyone to make you feed your baby somewhere else such as a bathroom and it is illegal for anyone to harass you for feeding your baby.

It's important to learn about your rights and be prepared to stand up for yourself just in case you need to, but fewer and fewer women are even having a problem with this so you probably will never have to. I, as well as many of my friends, have never had any issues or negative reactions when feeding our children in public.

Benefits of Breastfeeding That Crunchy Parents Understand

Breastmilk is a truly remarkable substance much greater than anything man could hope to create. It's often referred to as "liquid gold" and for good reason. Breastmilk is perfectly designed for your baby containing absolutely everything that their body needs not only to survive, but to thrive. It contains endless numbers of beneficial properties and is full of life. The benefits of breastfeeding that we have discovered are numerous and there are more benefits and properties of breastmilk that are still being discovered regularly.

__Breastmilk Changes__

As your baby grows, breastmilk changes to best provide for their changing needs. The milk that your body produces when your baby is first born is much different than the milk that your body produces when your baby is a couple of weeks old or a couple of months old or even a couple of years old. It doesn't just change as your baby ages either. Your milk changes to best suit the needs of your baby throughout the day and as conditions change and even when your baby gets sick.

For example, at nighttime, your body produces breastmilk that contains melatonin that helps your baby to sleep. If it's particularly hot outside, your body will produce milk with a higher water content to prevent your baby from becoming dehydrated. Your breastmilk is always passing antibodies to your baby, but if your baby is sick, your body produces extra antibodies specifically for whatever is ailing your baby.

Breastfed Babies Don't Get Sick as Often

Since your baby is constantly receiving antibodies through your breastmilk, it makes sense that they won't get sick as often. From the moment your baby is born, they are receiving large doses of antibodies through your breastmilk. The first milk that your body produces is called colostrum and it contains even higher concentrations of antibodies for your little one.

When you come into contact with an illness, your body immediately begins to make antibodies for the illness and passes them to your baby through your breastmilk to help prevent the baby from getting sick at all. However, even if your baby does get sick, they will likely not experience sickness as severe as they would if they were not breastfed and they will also likely get well more quickly thanks to their immune system receiving a nice boost from the breastmilk.

Once, when my son was only a few months old, my entire family got intensely sick, even my in-laws were very sick. My husband affectionately refers to it as "The Weekend from Hell". Throughout that weekend, and even into the week, we were all throwing up non-stop, struggling with diarrhea almost constantly, and just completely unable to eat or even function properly. Everyone, except our son, was completely miserable. He got a little sick, in fact, he was sick first, but he was still happily smiling throughout the whole weekend and experienced nothing like the symptoms that we suffered with.

Breastmilk is Free

This is one completely undeniable benefit of breastfeeding. Not only is breastmilk the perfect first food for your baby, but it comes at no cost! When people talk about how expensive babies are, one of the things they are likely thinking of is the cost of formula. Formula costs vary depending on type and brand but there is no question that it is costly no matter what. Formula is a constant reoccurring expense for at least the entire first year of your baby's life. You can potentially save thousands of dollars by choosing to breastfeed over formula feeding.

There can be some costs associated with breastfeeding, but they aren't always necessary and they still don't compare to the amount of money you would have to spend on formula if you choose it over breastmilk for your baby. The costs that may come along with breastfeeding are mostly in relation to pumping breastmilk.

If you need a pump because you work outside of the home as many mothers do, it can cost you up to a few hundred dollars. Although, there are much more affordable options available and insurance will often cover a breast pump. You may also have to buy bags or bottles to store breastmilk in. Any other costs associated with breastfeeding are generally very inconsequential and are typically not reoccurring. This would include things such as nipple cream when you are first starting your breastfeeding journey.

Benefits of Breastfeeding for the Mother

Your baby is not the only one that benefits from breastfeeding. Breastfeeding is very beneficial for you as well. Breastfeeding releases hormones that often give women a feeling of temporary euphoria which also aids in bonding with your baby. Breastfeeding also stimulates your uterus to continue contracting after birth (don't worry – these contractions are nothing like labor contractions) which helps the placenta to separate and emerge as well as helps prevent post-partum hemorrhage.

Breastfeeding has long-term benefits for the mother as well. In fact, research reveals that a woman's chance of feminine related cancers such as uterine cancer, cervical cancer, ovarian cancer, and of course, breast cancer is lowered by breastfeeding. It has even been shown that for each month of breastfeeding that the woman's chance of those cancers lowers further. Breastfeeding also burns a lot of calories which means that under the right conditions, breastfeeding can help you lose some of your pregnancy weight.

Other Benefits of Breastfeeding

There are many other benefits of breastfeeding as well. Studies show that breastfed babies tend to have higher IQs and that the length of breastfeeding plays a role in how high their IQ is as well. In other words, breastfeeding can make your baby smarter. Another nice benefit of breastfeeding is that the poo of breastfed babies has a much less offensive odor than that of their formula fed peers.

Actually, back when my husband and I were just dating, we babysat for a friend of his. I was having a blast caring for their baby, just imagining how amazing it would be when I could have my own. That is when she pooped. She was formula fed, and when we opened that diaper, I almost threw up. I had to leave the room, literally gagging, and my poor husband-to-be had to face it all alone. I cried and cried after that talking about how I could never be a mom because I couldn't even change a diaper. Fortunately, when my son was born, I was pleasantly surprised to find that his poo had almost no scent at all, and even the slight scent it did have, was not unpleasant.

Most breastfeeding women agree that overall, breastfeeding is easier than formula feeding. Breastfeeding is often as simple as lifting your shirt compared to having to get a clean bottle, measure formula, measure water, mix, and warm. Breastfeeding is especially simpler in the night when mothers are often able to feed their babies quickly and easily without even having the baby have to fully wake.

Breastmilk is also always available whereas in the case of emergencies or financial difficulties, formula may be harder to come by. When a baby is breastfed, the breastmilk plays a role similar to the placenta where it "programs" the baby's brain and therefore breastfeeding helps your baby achieve optimal brain development. Feeding a baby with breastmilk has also been shown to reduce the risk of obesity, allergies, diabetes, ear infections, and even SIDS, or Sudden Infant Death Syndrome.

Getting Off to a Good Start with Breastfeeding as a Crunchy Family

It's important to get off to a good start in your breastfeeding journey to help ensure a positive experience for everyone, reduce your chance of running into problems, and help you to meet your breastfeeding goals. There are some things that you can do to help you get off to the best start possible in your breastfeeding journey.

Educate Yourself

One of the most important things you can do to help make sure that you get a good start in your breastfeeding relationship is to educate yourself on breastfeeding. It's important to learn the ins and outs of breastfeeding. Learn about how your body works to produce milk, how your baby's latch affects breastfeeding, and about all the different things to expect when breastfeeding.

If possible, it is a great idea to take a breastfeeding class during your pregnancy. You'll be able to learn everything you need to know about breastfeeding your baby ahead of time and can ask any questions that you may have as well. Bringing your partner along with you to the class can also be very helpful when it comes to helping them provide you with the best support possible.

Start as Soon as Possible

To get off to a good start breastfeeding, you'll want to feed your baby as soon as possible after birth. Ideally, your baby should be placed on your chest immediately after birth for some very important skin-to-skin time. This is the perfect time to breastfeed your baby for the first time. Remember that you and your baby are designed to do this, and even if you don't get it perfect right away, that it will come with time.

Nurse on Demand

Something that a lot of women end up doing wrong, usually due to incorrect advice, is trying to put their breastfed baby on a schedule. Sometimes, a schedule may work for an older baby, but a young baby, especially a newborn, should never be put on a feeding schedule. Your baby's body knows exactly when it needs to eat and signals your baby of this. Your baby will let you know when they are hungry. They will not eat too much or too little if they are allowed to nurse on demand.

Nursing your baby on demand will also help you to establish a good milk supply that is adequate for your baby's needs. When a baby is first born, their stomach is tiny – only about the size of a marble. That means that it empties quickly so your baby will have to nurse often to remain satisfied and get an adequate amount of milk.

Luckily, the first milk that your body produces is a milk called colostrum that is highly concentrated in nutrients and antibodies to give your baby a great start. This first milk is golden-yellow in color and thicker than mature breastmilk. It contains everything your newborn needs and allows them to get plenty of much-needed nutrients from short but frequent feedings.

Your baby will need to nurse at least 8 times a day in the beginning but most likely will nurse much more than that. This is completely healthy and normal. Prepare for all the time that you will spend nursing by having plenty of healthy snacks on hand that are easily eaten with one hand. You will also need more water while breastfeeding, so it can be a good idea to have a refillable water bottle to keep with you as well.

It isn't necessary to measure your water intake as everyone will have different needs. Instead, just make sure that you are always drinking to thirst. Believe it or not, too much water can be a bad thing too. So, if you are thirsty, drink plenty of water, but don't force yourself to drink more than you actually are thirsty for. Your body knows what it needs.

Surround Yourself with Support

As with birth, it is also important to surround yourself with support for breastfeeding. Your partner should be your biggest source of support. They need to be educated in breastfeeding and understand how it works, why nursing on demand is important, and how they can help you.

Some ways that your partner can help you are by bringing you snacks and water as needed, taking the baby for a while in-between feedings to allow you to rest, doing some of the chores around the house that you would normally be doing, and of course being a source of emotional support. Your partner should be there to listen to you vent if you need to, help gently remind you why you chose to breastfeed if you are having troubles, and to stick up for you if you receive any negative reactions from others.

In addition to your partner, you should also let the rest of your family as well as close friends know, especially older children if this isn't your first baby, that you will be breastfeeding and what that entails. Let them know about the time that it will take, the importance and benefits of it, and that you need their support.

Seek Help When You Need It

One of the biggest reasons that many women never meet their breastfeeding goals is because they run into a problem and never seek help to try to solve that problem. Many of the problems that some breastfeeding mothers run into are very easy to solve, and even if it isn't an easy fix, there is almost always something you can do.

It's very important that if you are having issues of any type with breastfeeding that you seek help. The best place that you can go for help with breastfeeding problems is a lactation consultant. They are experts in the field of lactation whereas your OBGYN, primary care doctor, and child's pediatrician are likely unaware of how to properly diagnose and solve problems related to breastfeeding.

A lactation consultant will know exactly what they are doing and can help you to figure out exactly what is going on that is causing your problem. They can then help you to make a plan to solve the problem and get back on track towards your breastfeeding goals. They can teach you tips and tricks to help you avoid problems as well, so it isn't a bad idea to get in contact with and possibly meet with a lactation consultant before your baby is even born. My husband and I took a breastfeeding class given by a lactation consultant during my first pregnancy and it made such a difference for us.

Potential Problems and How Crunchy Moms Combat Them

Breastfeeding is natural and you and your baby are designed for it. However, that doesn't mean that it always comes easy. There can be problems that you run into during breastfeeding, but almost all of the problems that you may face can be solved and you can continue your nursing journey and still meet your breastfeeding goals. Many mothers report that they have trouble when they first start breastfeeding but that breastfeeding gets easier and easier for them as time goes on.

Poor Latch

Nipple pain and discomfort is probably the most common complaint of new breastfeeding moms and is almost always caused by poor latch, which can also cause a variety of other problems with breastfeeding. Unfortunately, many women think that this pain and discomfort is just a part of breastfeeding that women have to deal with. The good news is that isn't true at all. If nursing is causing you pain, something isn't right.

It's important for your baby to be latched on correctly to prevent pain. Proper latch is also important to make sure that your baby is getting enough milk. If your baby isn't latching correctly, they won't stimulate your breasts to make enough milk and your supply could drop. Low supply is another one of the common problems that some women experience and it is almost always due to poor latch. Low supply can also lead to inadequate weight gain in your baby.

To avoid problems of all kinds in your breastfeeding journey, you want to make sure that your baby is latching onto your breast properly. A proper latch is one of the most important things when it comes to ensuring successful breastfeeding. Your baby should take a full mouthful of breast into their mouth and their lips should be flared open when latched properly.

The roof of your baby's mouth consists of a soft palate and a hard palate. The hard palate is in the front of the mouth and the soft palate is in the back of the mouth. You should be able to use your tongue to feel both of these areas in your own mouth. If the baby is latched properly, your nipple will land in the back of their mouth with their soft palate. If your nipple lands against the hard palate it can cause you pain or discomfort. This can also lead to bleeding and cracked nipples which will cause further pain while nursing.

The easiest way to fix this problem as well as other problems caused by poor latch is simply to fix your baby's latch. Your lactation consultant can help teach both you and your baby proper latching techniques to ensure a good latch. Sometimes the bad latch may be caused by a tongue or lip tie. Both the lips and the tongue are tethered to the mouth by something called a frenulum.

If the frenulum is too short or tight, it can be restrictive to the tongue or lips. If your baby has an upper lip tie or a tongue tie, it can prevent them from latching properly. This can usually be fixed by a simple and mostly painless procedure where the tie is released either by snipping it or using a laser. Your lactation consultant can diagnose a tie as well as recommend a professional that can release the tie if necessary.

In some cases, such as with a lip or tongue tie, it may be recommended to you to use a nipple shield either to allow healing or as a temporary solution until the real problem can be fixed. A nipple shield is a piece of silicone that you place over your nipple before your baby latches. It protects your nipple from receiving further damage and allows it to heal more easily. It has small holes in it just like a bottle nipple that allow the milk to pass through to your baby.

Engorgement, Clogged Ducts, and Mastitis

Another common problem that some breastfeeding mothers run into is engorgement. This occurs when the breasts become very full of milk. It can be very uncomfortable and in some cases painful. Most new mothers experience this when their mature breastmilk begins to come in at around 3 to 5 days after their baby is born. This is normal and will start to go away shortly once your milk supply starts to regulate. Engorgement can also happen after your supply regulates if you go too long without nursing or pumping on one or both sides.

Engorgement can lead to another very common problem that many breastfeeding women may experience called clogged ducts. These can occur when a blockage occurs somewhere in the milk ducts in your breasts. Milk builds up behind the blockage and causes pain, redness, tenderness, and often a lump in your breast. If not taken care of quickly, clogged ducts can lead to a serious infection of the breast known as mastitis.

When dealing with a clogged duct, it's best to nurse as much as possible on the affected side. However, you should be careful not to stop nursing on the other side either because that could cause a clogged duct to occur on that side as well. Encourage your baby to nurse often and massage the affected area at the time of nursing. You can also take a hot shower and massage the area as well as hand express milk while the hot water runs over your affected breast.

You can try a heat pack on the affected breast shortly before nursing sessions, and you can try something called dangle nursing. That means you lay your baby somewhere such as your bed and get down on your hands and knees above the baby. You then allow your breast to "dangle" down above your baby and nurse them in that position. This allows gravity to help loosen the clog.

If you aren't able to get rid of your clogged duct quickly enough, you may develop mastitis. Symptoms of mastitis include a high fever, severe pain in the affected breast, aches and pains throughout your entire body, weakness, and fatigue. These symptoms often come on very quickly. For this reason, you should contact your health care provider as soon as you suspect that you may have mastitis.

I got mastitis once, and I was so weak and disorientated, that I quickly realized I couldn't care for my son properly. I called my husband to come home from work (this was before he quit his job so we could both work from home) and I put my son in a baby carrier and sat down outside. I knew I didn't trust myself to hold my son without the carrier, and I knew that I couldn't walk around either. By sitting outside, I was able to keep him content until my husband came to help me.

If you do develop mastitis, you will require antibiotics to fight the infection. This is because without treatment, the infection can be very serious and can even be fatal. Fortunately, this is not a concern because treatment is simple and easy. You can usually get a prescription for antibiotics for mastitis from your obstetrician. They should give you a prescription that is safe for breastfeeding, but always double check to be sure. You may also want to take a probiotic while you're on the antibiotics to help combat possible side effects from them such as diarrhea.

Crunchy Families Practice Full-Term Breastfeeding

One thing that most crunchy families tend to do that others often don't is practice full-term breastfeeding. It is often considered to be extended breastfeeding if you continue nursing your baby past the age of one year because it is beyond the normal in our modern society. However, a more appropriate term is "full-term breastfeeding". This is because the word "extended" suggests beyond what is biologically normal.

Following what is biologically normal is a huge part of being a crunchy parent, so it only makes sense that a crunchy parent would allow their child to self-wean. When a child is allowed to wean on their own terms, they will usually stop nursing somewhere between 2 and 7 years old depending on a number of factors.

One of those factors is the child's access to other foods, so in our society where we tend to have plenty to eat, most children that self-wean won't go past 4 years or so. Children over a year old also tend to nurse much less often and most children will go down to nursing only once a day or once every few days before they wean completely.

Some people claim that there is no benefit to breastfeeding beyond the first year or two of a child's life. Research does not support this claim at all, though. Breastmilk does not suddenly lose its benefits when a child turns a certain age. Breastmilk is beneficial indefinitely. It is especially beneficial for a child that has not fully developed their immune system yet. The immune system isn't fully developed until around 7 years or so of age.

Crunchy Alternative Uses of Breastmilk

One particularly crunchy practice is using breastmilk for more than just feeding your baby. Interestingly enough, breastmilk has many amazing properties that give it tons of wonderful uses beyond just feeding the baby.

Healing Uses of Breastmilk

One of the most amazing things about breastmilk beyond providing sustenance for your baby, is it's healing properties. Breastmilk tends to kill bad bacteria while leaving beneficial bacteria alone while also promoting healing. For this reason, it can help to prevent infection and even treat certain infections.

If you or your child gets a scrape or a cut, you can use breastmilk on it rather than using something like antibiotic ointment. This will help prevent the injury from becoming infected and promote faster healing. Many people also swear by breastmilk in the treatment of burns. Breastmilk can even be very beneficial for severe burns and help promote faster healing as well as help to soothe pain.

Another common alternative healing use of breastmilk is to treat conjunctivitis, commonly known as pink eye. It is a surprisingly effective treatment that you can use in place of other eye drops or antibiotics. To use breastmilk to treat pink eye, simply place a drop or two in each eye several times a day and you should see results quickly. It will also be soothing to itchy and irritated eyes. For this reason, it can also be used as regular eye drops to help treat itchy, dry, or irritated eyes. It can even help reduce the appearance of red eyes.

Breastmilk can also be used to help heal ear infections. It is most effective when used early on at the start of an infection. Use it often in the ears for best results. Ear infections can become serious and progress quickly, so it may be necessary in some cases to use further treatment in place of or in addition to the breastmilk.

Another great healing use of breastmilk is for diaper rash. Simply apply a thin layer of breastmilk to the affected area after wiping at diaper changes. Allow it to air dry before replacing the diaper. The breastmilk will promote healing, but it can also be a good idea to use a water barrier in addition to the breastmilk to help prevent the rash from getting worse. A great natural and very crunchy choice for a water barrier for a diaper rash is coconut oil. Just add a thin layer of coconut oil to the affected area after the breastmilk dries.

If you are like many other mothers, you may find that you suffer from post-partum acne. Breastmilk can be a very effective treatment for that as well. Simply apply a little breastmilk to the acne a few times each day and you will probably start noticing improvement within a couple days. It can also help to prevent acne. Similarly, it can be used to help treat eczema and cradle cap.

Milk Baths

Something that a lot of crunchy families use breastmilk for other than feeding their baby is to give their baby a milk bath. Milk baths can have many benefits for your baby's skin. It can help to combat any skin problems that they may have such as rashes, eczema and any other irritations of the skin. Milk baths are also soothing, moisturizing and rejuvenating. You may even want to take one after feeling how soft and healthy your baby's skin is after a milk bath.

To give your baby a milk bath is very simple. You simply add some of your milk to their bath water. There is no exact amount that you have to use, but generally you want to give the water a nice cloudy appearance. If you are limited on how much spare milk you have, you can use something smaller than the full-size tub to bathe your baby so that the milk is more concentrated. Other than adding the milk, you'll just bathe your baby as you normally would.

Cooking with Breastmilk

Some people may find it bizarre, but some crunchy families use breastmilk in some of their cooking and baking in place of other milks such as cow's milk. It is a much healthier option compared to any other kind of milk. It is designed specifically for humans and has many healthy properties such as immune boosting antibodies, and a little bit of literally everything that humans need to survive.

Unless you have time to pump all the time, in addition to feeding your baby, you probably won't want to use breastmilk in all of your recipes. However, it can be a great alternative for smaller uses such as coffee creamer. It is also great to know that you can use breastmilk in a pinch if you are out of whatever other type of milk that your recipe may call for. You could actually even make special ice cream or other treats for your baby using breastmilk if you wanted to.

Breastmilk Products

Finally, you can also use breastmilk to make products with. Believe it or not, there is actually a market for these products. You can find all sorts of recipes online, or you can just make your own up. Some of the things that some crunchy parents use breastmilk to make include soap, lotion, and conditioner. Breastmilk is very good for the skin and can be very moisturizing. Just make sure to not make too much at a time because it will go bad much faster than commercially made products.

Chapter 3: Crunchy Diet

Crunchy families are generally very health conscious and that means being careful about what they put into their bodies and their babies' bodies. For this reason, it's generally considered crunchy to try to have a diet that consists of mostly natural foods with no preservatives, no added hormones, no artificial colors, and with minimal or no added sugars.

Crunchy parents also avoid giving their baby solid foods too soon. Many times, babies are given baby food as early as 3 or 4 months. Some babies even receive things like rice cereals as early as a few weeks old. Research shows that this is much too early and can have some serious negative effects for your little one.

Unfortunately, it often takes doctor's offices many years to catch up to current research, so many doctors are still recommending things other than breastmilk (or formula) to babies under the age of six months. Six months is the earliest that your baby should be receiving anything other than breastmilk or formula.

In addition to being six months old, your baby should have good trunk control so that they are able to easily sit up on their own, they should show genuine interest in foods that you are eating, they should be able to grasp things with their hands, and they should have lost the reflex to automatically push things out of their mouth using their tongue.

Up until at least a year old, breastmilk should still be their main source of nutrition. For this reason, when introducing solids to your baby, you should always nurse them before trying other foods to make sure that other foods don't replace their much-needed nutrition from breastmilk.

Crunchy Families Practice Baby-Led Weaning

One common practice of crunchy families when it comes to diet is practicing something known as baby-led weaning. This is basically when you feed your baby regular foods that you are already eating rather than giving them purees that are specifically made for babies. There are many benefits to baby-led weaning and it is considered a more natural approach to introducing your baby to solids.

Baby-led weaning exposes your baby to a variety of flavors and textures from a very young age. This helps to produce children that like a variety of foods and are much less picky eaters in most cases. It is also much easier because your baby will feed themselves when baby-led weaning rather than you having to sit there and spoon-feed them. This saves time as you can eat at the same time as your baby and it is much easier to clean up after regular foods compared to purees.

This will also help your baby to develop fine motor skills and teach them to chew before swallowing. It is best for them to learn to chew at this young age because young babies have a gag reflex that is closer to the front of the mouth. This helps them to learn that they have to chew before swallowing which actually helps avoid choking.

Baby-led weaning also saves money because instead of buying specific food just for your baby, you can just give them a little bit of whatever you and your family are already having. You should, of course, still avoid obvious choking hazards such as nuts, grapes, and cherry tomatoes. Grapes and cherry tomatoes can be sliced long-ways before given to baby to help prevent choking. Other foods should be cut in a way that allows baby to easily grip the food and feed themselves. Cutting into strips works for most foods.

Many people are surprised to find that babies over the age of 6 months are able to safely eat everything that adults eat apart from honey. It's best to wait until your baby is at least a year old before introducing honey, but everything else is free game. Just make sure that you cut foods in a way that prevents choking and allows your child to easily grip the food.

Don't worry if your baby is eating much right away. They will start to eat more over time. If they don't have teeth or many teeth yet, they may simply gum the foods for now and might not swallow a lot. Some babies start out by chewing foods and then spitting them out without actually swallowing much. This is normal and no reason to be concerned. Your baby should be getting all of their needs met through breastmilk still and even so, your baby will still be getting some nutrition simply by sucking and chewing on foods.

My son didn't eat much at all the first couple months after he turned 6 months old, even though we offered regularly. After a couple months, he started to chew on foods a lot but usually spit them out. When he first started eating watermelon, he would chew the watermelon and suck all the juice out, then spit it all out. He loved the stuff and still does actually, but back then, we would pull him out of his high chair and then have to scrape up a massive pile of watermelon mush. It was still easier than cleaning up purees though and we got a kick out of it. Even though he didn't really start eating solids regularly until 13-14 months, he was very healthy and remains so to this day.

Making Your Own Baby Food as a Crunchy Parent

Baby-led weaning has many benefits, but it just isn't for everyone, even if you are a crunchy parent. Luckily, there is another crunchy alternative to the traditional store-bought baby food. That alternative is to make your own home-made baby purees. It takes more work and time, and is also more expensive but it is also definitely healthier, more natural, and crunchier than the store-bought purees.

To make your own baby foods at home, you can use a food processor or a blender to puree fresh foods of all kinds for your baby. You can try all sorts of different combinations for your baby to try. It's usually a good idea to make larger sized batches at a time and store them to have on hand as you need them. Glass jars are a great way to store your home-made baby food.

Eating Organic is Essential with a Crunchy Lifestyle

Crunchy and organic go hand in hand. Organic eating is much more natural, healthy, and safe. Organic foods are produced more naturally. They are free of most pesticides and other dangerous chemicals that often come along with conventionally produced foods. Organic foods are also non-GMO which is another important factor when choosing a healthier, more natural, and of course, crunchy diet for you and your family.

Organic Food is Safer

Foods that are not organic are produced using many pesticides, genetic modification, unnatural hormones, and other potentially dangerous chemicals and additives. All of these things can be dangerous and affect your body in negative ways. This is especially true since you are exposed to it all repeatedly in the foods that you eat.

Organic Food is Healthier

In addition to being free of many dangerous substances found in traditionally produced foods, organic foods have higher levels of nutrients that are important to our bodies. Studies show that the level of things like flavonoids in organic foods are higher than in foods that are not produced organically. Meats that are farmed organically also tend to have higher levels of omega-3 fatty acids which are essential for proper brain development.

Organic Food is More Environmentally Friendly

It makes sense that the more natural practice of organic farming is better for the environment and the Earth than conventional farming. Organic farming helps to reduce pesticides and other dangerous substances in the environment and helps to promote healthier soil, healthier water, and much less toxic waste than conventional farming. Crunchy families tend to be more concerned about the environment than many others so it makes sense that they would support the organic farming industry as well.

Chapter 4: How Crunchy Parents Diaper Their Babies

Another practice that is almost always associated with crunchy parenting is cloth diapering. There is no denying the many amazing benefits that are associated with cloth diapering, but many people choose not to do it because they often don't realize how far cloth diapers have come over the years. I remember when I first heard of someone cloth diapering in modern times and I was shocked and confused. I kind of thought my friend was crazy, but I was also intrigued.

Often times, when people think of cloth diapers, they probably think of the large white squares of fabric, diaper pins, and plastic pants. Luckily, modern cloth diapers really have come a long way. There are now some cloth diapers that are just as easy and simple as disposable diapers. When I learned this, I decided to look more into it and eventually got my husband to reluctantly agree to go to a Cloth Diapers 101 class. A few days later, we bought a whole stash of cloth diapers. This was one of the few crunchy things that I really had to work to sell my husband on. However, 2 years later, he is now a strong advocate for cloth diapering!

Benefits That Crunchy Parents Get from Cloth Diapering

There are many different benefits that can be gained from cloth diapering, and every parent seems to have a different reason for choosing cloth diapers over disposable ones. I was initially interested in cloth diapers because I liked that it was different and they were cute. Once I realized how much money could be saved, I was sold. Since then, I've learned about the many other benefits of cloth diapering and am happier than ever with our decision to make the switch when our first baby was 3 months old.

Cloth Diapers Are Better for the Environment

One of the crunchiest reasons that crunchy parents tend to choose cloth diapers is because they are the greener, more environmentally friendly choice. Babies go through several thousand diaper changes throughout their first year alone. If you're using disposables, every diaper change adds waste to a landfill.

Disposable diapers also take an extremely long time to decompose. It has been estimated that it could take up to 500 years for a disposable diaper to decompose – that is half of a millennium! Not to mention that the production of disposable diapers is much more damaging to the environment than that of cloth diapers.

Cloth Diapers Save Money

A huge benefit of cloth diapering is all the money that you can save by doing it. Disposable diapers are often the highest cost for parents during the first couple of years of their child's life if they choose not to cloth diaper. You can save literally thousands of dollars by cloth diapering. That is especially true considering that cloth diapers can be reused with each child you have and can even be resold once you are finished with them.

Cloth Diapers Are Safer for Your Baby

Another important benefit of cloth diapers is that they are safer for your baby. The materials used in cloth diapers are generally more natural and safer for your little one's sensitive skin compared to chemical-laden disposable diapers that expose your baby to chemicals 24/7 for usually the first couple of years of their life.

Cloth Diapers Are Cuter

This isn't exactly a crunchy reason to cloth diaper, but it certainly adds to how awesome cloth diapers are. Cloth diapers come in tons of different colors, styles, and prints. If you can think of it, there is a cloth diaper out there of it. Disposables are thin and cheap looking and usually are plain with the same simple design on every single diaper. Cloth diapers are adorable and you can even match them to your baby's clothing for even more cuteness.

Types of Cloth Diapers for Crunchy Parents to Choose From

Since the cloth diaper has evolved so much, there are now multiple different types of diapers to choose from. Some are extremely similar to the old-fashioned cloth diapers, while some are now designed as simple as possible just like disposable diapers. Each different type of diaper has different benefits and drawbacks compared to the others.

Flats and Prefolds

These are the type of diapers that are very similar in design to the more old-fashioned type of cloth diapers. Flats are large white squares of fabric that you fold into the shape of a diaper and then fasten onto your baby. You can use old-fashioned diaper pins if you prefer, but there are also modern fasteners that are easier and safer that you can use instead.

Prefolds work much the same way as flats, but the only difference is, that as their name suggests, they are partially folded already and sewn that way. This makes them slightly easier to use than flats. These types of cloth diapers do require some kind of cover to be waterproof. The biggest benefit to flats and prefolds is that they are the least expensive option for diapering your baby.

Contours and Fitteds

These diapers are a step up from prefolds. They are made much like prefolds, but they are already shaped like a diaper so that they do not require any folding. Fitteds have elastic around the back of the diaper and the legs of the diaper to get a better fit and sometimes they also have snap closures so that you don't have to use a diaper fastener like with flats, prefolds, and contours. These diaper types also require a cover to be waterproof. They are easier and more convenient than flats and prefolds, but come at a higher price.

Pocket Diapers

These are the face of modern cloth diapering. They are a diaper shell that is made of two different layers – a water resistant outer layer and a stay-dry inner layer. They are designed to have an absorbent cloth insert placed inside the "pocket" between the two layers. The inserts that you can use with pocket diapers come in many different materials and styles to choose from.

These diapers do not require covers, making them easier, quicker, and more convenient to use than the previously discussed diaper types. They close using either snaps or hook and loop closures, commonly known as Velcro. These diapers are a nice mix of convenience and affordability.

Hybrid Fitteds

Hybrid fitteds are very similar to fitted diapers but have one major difference – they don't require covers because they have a water-resistant layer that is usually hidden under a cute print. They typically close via snaps. They are a favorite of many crunchy parents because they are very effective and easy as well as come in nearly unlimited prints and styles. However, they are usually the most expensive cloth diapering option. Although, they are still less expensive than disposables in the long run.

All-in-Ones and All-in-Twos

Another very popular option amongst cloth diapering families are all-in-ones (AIOs) and all-in-twos (AI2s). These diapers are similar to pocket diapers, only AIOs have the insert sewn into them, and AI2s have inserts that snap into place in the shell. AIOs are probably the cloth diapers most similar to disposable diapers. Both AIOs and AI2s are very simple to use and close using either snaps or hook and loop closures. They are usually less expensive than hybrid fitteds, but a little pricier than pockets or other cheaper options.

Cloth Diaper Covers

If you choose to use a type of diaper that requires a diaper cover, you will also need to choose a type of diaper cover since there are several different options to choose from. The most common type of diaper cover is a PUL cover, or Polyurethane Laminate. It is a thin diaper cover that closes using snaps or hook and loop closures. It is the least breathable type of cover but is generally very affordable and can be washed in your regular diaper routine.

There are also wool covers and fleece covers. Wool covers are often chosen because they are completely natural. They are the most expensive type of cover and also require special care outside of your normal wash routine. However, they do require less frequent cleaning and many people are able to get by with only 2 wool covers. Fleece covers are kind of in-between. They are not natural the way that the wool covers are and typically are not quite as effective as wool, but they are less expensive. They also require more frequent washing but can be washed in your regular wash routine. In most cases, wool and fleece covers are pull-up style, but in some cases, may close using snaps.

Crunchy Parents Need to Know How to Care for Cloth Diapers

One thing that often holds some parents, even some crunchy parents, back from cloth diapering is the intimidation factor. They are worried that it will be too difficult or time consuming or even too gross to care for their cloth diapers. However, if you do it correctly, none of these things are true. It is very easy to incorporate care of cloth diapers into your normal routine. My husband was very worried about all of these things, but he now willingly does about 90% of the diaper laundry for our 2 kids with no complaints at all.

Storing Used Diapers Until Wash Day

When cloth diapering, you will need a good way to store your baby's used diapers until you have enough diapers to do a wash. You want to make sure that you wash a fair amount of diapers together because if your washer is too empty, the diapers won't agitate well and may not get as clean as they should. The best way to store used cloth diapers until washing time is in a diaper pail lined with a pail liner.

Cloth diaper pail liners are made of water resistant materials and are able to be washed right along with your diapers. You can buy an actual diaper pail, or you can use a small trash can or hamper that you put a diaper pail liner into. It is a good idea to have at least 2 pail liners so that you can rotate them during washing. It is also best to have a set up where your diapers get some air. If your diapers are closed off, they will begin to develop a strong odor.

When you change your baby's diaper, you can place any diapers that have urine only on them straight into the diaper pail to wait for washing. If your baby has a bowel movement in the diaper, the way that you deal with it will depend on your baby's diet. If your baby is exclusively breastfed, meaning that they consume absolutely nothing other than breastmilk, you can put their dirty diapers straight into the diaper pail as well. This is because breastmilk poo is water soluble.

If your baby is consuming anything other than breastmilk, such as formula or solid foods, you will need to first remove the poo from the diaper before placing it into the diaper pail because it is not safe to put it straight into the washer. This is what scares some people away from cloth diapering, but it really isn't so bad, especially if you have the right tools.

To remove poo from a diaper, there are several methods to choose from. You can do the classic "dunk and swish" method which is quick and doesn't require any extra tools. To do this, you simply dip the diaper into the toilet and swish it around until the poo comes off. Fortunately, if that isn't your style, there are some other methods you can use as well. In some cases, specifically once your baby is eating more solid foods, you will be able to simply "plop" the poo into the toilet. Another method is to use something such as a spatula to scrape the poo into the toilet. Make sure you label that spatula, though.

Probably the easiest and most popular method of removing poo from a cloth diaper is using a diaper sprayer. This is a hose with a sprayer on the end that attaches directly to your toilet. You use it to spray the poo off into the toilet. You can also buy something called a sprayer shield to make the process even easier and avoid splashing. This is a product that the diaper clips onto and then you spray the diaper through the shield which avoids getting water and poo everywhere.

Washing Diapers

Once you get enough diapers to do a wash, you can simply dump your diaper pail into the washer. You don't want to go more than a week max between washes or your diapers will begin to smell very bad and they can begin to mildew. Ideally, you should aim to wash every 2 to 4 days. You will need to first run a pre-wash on your diapers before doing a main wash.

To do a pre-wash, add a small amount of detergent and do a short wash cycle on your diapers. Once the pre-wash is finished, you will want to add enough detergent for a typical large load of laundry. Then you should run a long, heavy-duty wash cycle. As long as you do everything correctly, the temperature of the water won't matter. You should never use fabric softener with your cloth diapers as this can cause the diapers to repel liquid rather than absorb it.

Drying Diapers

Drying diapers is pretty straight forward and you can really choose to do it however you want to. Many crunchy parents choose to line dry their diapers, but others may not have a good set up or climate to do that in or they may just prefer not to. If you choose to dry your diapers in the dryer, there are just a few simple rules to follow.

First, you should never use dryer sheets with your diapers since they can cause your diapers to repel rather than absorb. The only other thing is that if you choose to dry your diapers using heat, you should allow the diapers to cool completely before using them. This is because if you stretch the elastics while they are hot, they will wear out and relax faster.

Chapter 5: Babywearing is a Hallmark of Crunchy Parenting

Babywearing is an ancient practice carried on by generation after generation. It is the practice of using a piece of cloth or other specialized device to secure your baby or young child to your body in a way that allows you to hold your baby close while leaving your hands free. It is characterized as a crunchy parenting practice in today's society. This is likely because it helps to facilitate good attachment between a baby and their parents which is a big part of natural, crunchy parenting.

Babywearing has been an absolute Godsend for our family. When I say that I don't know how people parent without babywearing, I am dead serious. It has gotten us through all of the hardest times of parenting that we have encountered so far and does so much to help us on a daily basis. As far as material possessions go, nothing is more important to me than my carriers. Both my husband and I wear both of our kids every single day for various reasons and I really don't know what we would do without babywearing.

Benefits of Babywearing that Crunchy Parents Get

It's unnatural for a mother to be away from her baby, especially in the first weeks and months. Your baby has spent their entire existence in your body being protected by you and the last thing they want is to be separated from you now. Babywearing provides an easy way to safely keep your baby close to you and allows you and your baby to enjoy many other benefits as well.

Worn Babies Cry Less

One very useful benefit of babywearing is that babies that are worn tend to cry less than other babies. I can't even count the number of times that I've been complimented on my super happy, content kids while they were snugly wrapped against me. Not only does babywearing help you keep your baby nice and close on your chest – right where they want to be, but it also encases them in the comfortable snugness of the baby carrier. Both of these things work together to replicate feelings of being inside the womb which helps to soothe your baby as well as keep them feeling safe and secure.

In addition to keeping your baby feeling safe and secure, wearing them also helps you to be more in tune to your baby's needs. More often than not, if you keep your baby close, such as by wearing them, you will be able to quickly recognize their needs and respond to them before their discomfort escalates to crying. This will help to lower stress levels for both you and your baby. It also does a great job at boosting your confidence as a parent as well as your baby's trust in you.

Babywearing Frees Your Hands

Having a baby can make accomplishing anything other than caring for the baby difficult. Babies, especially very young babies, require constant love and attention. Most babies prefer to be held most of the time and understandably so. Unfortunately, that can make other aspects of life more difficult. It can be hard to even get simple tasks like laundry done when you have a baby.

Babywearing can help a ton with these things. It allows you to keep your little one nice and safe on your body without tying up your hands. When you wear your baby, you can accomplish all sorts of things that you wouldn't be able to if you were simply holding your baby. Everything from doing dishes and folding clothes to working on a computer or walking the dog can be made much simpler with babywearing.

Babywearing is Convenient

Going out with a baby can be difficult and sometimes complicated. If you are going to an event or even just out to the grocery store, you probably don't want to be holding your baby the entire time. Even a newborn can begin to feel heavy once you've held them for a while. Many parents may opt to bring a stroller along to put their baby in, but many babies either don't like the stroller or only want to remain in it for a short time. If that's the case, you may end up with a baby to carry and a stroller to push.

Strollers can be especially inconvenient when you're shopping since you'll usually have to push the stroller around in addition to a shopping cart. Babywearing eliminates the need to bring a stroller and typically keeps your baby happy while freeing your hands to push a cart or whatever else you may need them for while out and about. A baby carrier is also much lighter and takes up much less room than a stroller. Of course, there is nothing wrong with strollers and many parents choose to have both a stroller and a baby carrier to use depending on the situation.

Babywearing Helps to Keep Your Baby Safe

There are some situations where wearing your baby helps to keep them safe. For example, if you have a newborn, you'll want to be careful about what they are exposed to. It can be hard to keep hands and faces away from our delicate newborns, but babywearing can help with that.

Whether you are at a family gathering or dealing with strangers in public, having your baby in a carrier can help prevent people from breathing on and touching your baby as much. For one thing, your baby is harder for others to access when they are in the carrier, but it is also less likely for people to try to get close to your baby if they have to invade your personal space to do so.

If you are in a crowded area, babywearing may be safer than a stroller since your baby is right up against you where they are less likely to be bumped or bothered by other people. If you have an older baby or toddler, wearing them rather than allowing them to walk keeps them right next to you and allows them to have a better view. This also prevents your little one from becoming lost.

Types of Baby Carriers for Crunchy Parents to Choose From

Baby carriers come in many different forms. Each type of carrier varies greatly and each person finds a different type of carrier easiest or most preferable to use. Choosing the baby carrier that is right for you can be a difficult task, especially if you are unable to try it out personally before purchasing. However, learning about the most popular and common carriers can be helpful in making a decision.

Many areas also have babywearing groups and many babywearing groups have lending libraries. A babywearing lending library is a collection of different baby carriers that can be lent out to members of the babywearing group. This can be a great way to help you decide which type of baby carrier is right for you and your baby. You can also learn so much from your local babywearing group. I went to my first babywearing meeting when my son was just under a month old and I have come such a long way from there that I am now actually a leader within that group.

Pouch Slings

A pouch sling is an exceptionally simple baby carrier. It is simply a piece of fabric with one end sewn to the other to create a continuous loop. The sling is placed on the wearer's torso with one side over one shoulder and the other below the other shoulder. The baby is then simply slipped into the sling on the wearer's chest. They sit in it like a seat with their knees bent at the bottom rail of fabric and their lower legs and feet hanging out.

Pouch slings have the benefit of being extremely quick and simple but unlike other carriers, they are not adjustable. This means that you must get a specific size to fit you and your baby which also means that your baby will only be able to fit into it for a fairly short time before you would need to get a larger size. Generally, pouch slings are best used with young babies.

Ring Slings

Ring slings are similar to pouch slings in how they fit onto the wearer and baby. However, they consist of a longer piece of fabric and two rings that are typically made of metal but occasionally they may be plastic. Instead of the first end being sewn to the second like with pouch slings, the first end has the rings sewn into it and the second end is then thread through the rings.

Ring slings are slightly more complicated to use than pouch slings, but most wearers do learn how to use them quickly. They also have the benefit of adjustability allowing them to grow with your baby and hold not only newborns and young babies but also larger babies and even toddlers.

Stretchy Wraps

Stretchy wraps are a very popular choice for wearing newborns. They tend to have a weight limit around 30 lbs. but most people choose to discontinue use before reaching the weight limit due to comfort reasons. A stretchy wrap is one long piece of thin and stretchy fabric. To use it, you wrap it around yourself in a specific way and then put your baby into it, tighten it around your baby, and then tie the ends together. With young babies, these wraps are very comfortable and do an amazing job at making your baby feel nice and secure.

Soft Structured Carriers (SSCs)

Soft structured carriers or SSCs, also sometimes known as buckle carriers, are very user-friendly carriers. They consist of a panel that holds your baby against you and a waist strap and backpack-style shoulder straps to hook the carrier onto your body. The straps are adjustable to fit a range of sizes and use buckles to easily hook around you. They are generally best used with older babies or toddlers, but many

SSCs have a way to adapt the carrier to fit small babies or newborns.

Mei Tais

A mei tai is a traditional Asian carrier. It's sort of like a combination of a wrap and an SSC. It works a lot like an SSC, only instead of having buckles, it has straps that you wrap around yourself and tie to secure your baby. They can be just slightly more challenging than an SSC, but are still quick and easy plus they come with the extra comfort and style of a wrap.

Woven Wraps

Woven wraps are just like stretchy wraps in that they are one long piece of fabric that you use to wrap around yourself and your baby in order to secure the baby to your body. The biggest difference is that woven wraps are made of stronger material that has little to no give. They also come in large varieties of different lengths, widths, fabrics, colors, and designs.

Woven wraps are, without a doubt, the most versatile of all baby carriers. They can be used to wear babies and children of any age and size. There have even been adults that have used them to wear other adults just to prove that it could be done. There are endless different carries that can be done using a woven wrap as well. A single woven wrap can even be used to tandem wear – that is wear two children at once.

Babywearing Safety is a Must When Parenting Crunchy

Babywearing is very safe when done properly, but if done improperly, it can pose a serious risk to your baby's well-being. When it comes to the basic safety rules of babywearing, there are several things that you should always follow to ensure your baby is safe. There is actually a very well-known acronym in the babywearing community to help you remember these important safety rules of babywearing. That acronym is T.I.C.K.S.

Tight

When babywearing, you always want to make sure that the carrier you use fits very snugly around you and your precious baby. It should be tight enough that your baby isn't slouching down or able to do so. Your baby should be pressed closely right up against you.

In Sight

Another important rule of babywearing is that you should always be able to see your baby's face when you are wearing them. You want to have your baby's nose and mouth specifically always in your sight. Obviously, if you are wearing your baby on your back, it will be more difficult to see their face, and generally it's less of a concern because most wearers, especially new and inexperienced wearers, shouldn't wear younger babies on their backs. You should still be able to easily see their face using a mirror, though.

Close Enough to Kiss

This is another one that is a little different for back carries. It mostly applies to front carries, especially since where your baby is on your back can vary a good bit depending on what carry you are doing. When you are wearing your baby on your front, it is a good general rule to keep them high enough that you can easily kiss their head.

Keep Chin Off Chest

This is probably one of the most important things to remember when babywearing, especially when wearing a newborn baby. You need to always make sure that your baby's chin is off their chest. When their neck is bent to where their chin is touching their chest, it can actually close their airway.

Supported Back

This rule of babywearing goes along with keeping the carrier tight. No matter what type of carrier you use with your baby, you should always make sure that there is some part of the baby carrier that supports your baby's back well. Even when your baby is completely relaxed, they shouldn't end up slouching down in the carrier at all.

Babywearing Safety in High or Low Temperatures

In addition to the general rules that you should follow when babywearing, there are also some important tips that you should follow if you are babywearing in high or low temperatures. Babywearing in lower temperatures is pretty self-explanatory, so these tips will apply mostly to when babywearing in higher temperatures. If you are babywearing in lower temperatures, simply dress your baby appropriately for the weather before wearing them and continue to follow T.I.C.K.S.

Babywearing when it's hot is different because you have two bodies pressed against each other and your baby is covered by the baby carrier further trapping heat. Start by dressing your baby in thin and light clothing. You can even put them in just a diaper if you prefer. Remember that if you are feeling very hot and uncomfortable, they are probably feeling the same way. Take breaks from babywearing regularly if it's very hot so that your baby doesn't get overheated.

Provide your baby with regular access to breastmilk when it's hot, or if they are 6 months or older, you can provide them with water as well. This will help them to stay hydrated in the heat. Keep your baby shaded from the sun as much as possible to prevent sunburns and help to avoid getting too hot. You can use a sun hat or even an umbrella to shade your baby.

Basic Carries in a Woven Wrap for Crunchy Parents to Learn

Woven wraps, while the most versatile of baby carriers, have a learning curve to them. There are endless numbers of ways that you can use the wrap to carry your baby. You can use woven wraps for any size child and you can use them to do front carries, back carries, hip carries, and you can even use them to tandem carry two children at once.

Woven wraps also come in a variety of sizes, the size of a wrap is determined by its length. Each person has a base size which helps them determine what types of carries they can do with wraps of different sizes. Your base size is the size of wrap that you require to do a basic front carry known as a front wrap cross carry. This is typically considered the most basic carry in a woven wrap and its usually the first carry that most people learn. It is very similar to the way you wrap with a stretchy wrap.

The most common base size is a size 6 woven wrap which is 4.6 meters in length. However, it is not uncommon for someone to have a base size of 5 or 7. With your base size, you will be able to do all sorts of different carries, but if you want to do something more complex or possibly something showier, you might want a wrap longer than your base size. Alternatively, if you want to go with more simple carries, especially simple back carries, you might prefer a wrap shorter than your base size.

Familiarize yourself with the different parts of a woven wrap using the graphic below in order to more easily understand the following tutorials.

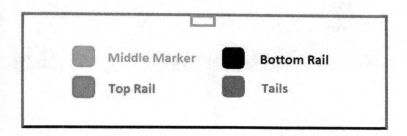

Front Wrap Cross Carry

Again, the front wrap cross carry, sometimes simply referred to as FWCC, is among the most simple and easy to learn carries in a woven wrap. Most people start out with learning this carry and it will be even easier to learn if you've used a stretchy wrap in the past.

Step 1: Start with the middle marker at the center of your chest. Take the top rail of the wrap in your left hand and wrap it around your back, bringing it forward over your right shoulder. Be careful not to twist the wrap at all. Now, repeat with the opposite side to match the bottom right picture below. This creates a pocket for your baby on the front of your chest and an "X" on your back. You can pull slightly on the rails of the wrap to tighten this pocket some before putting your baby in. This will make it easier to tighten once your baby is in the wrap.

Step 2: Place your baby with their belly against you up on your shoulder and pull the wrap up over your baby's back. Pull the bottom rail up so that their feet and lower legs are out of the wrap. Now, take the bottom rail and tuck it up in-between you and your baby. Then you can slide your baby down to the center of your chest. The bottom rail should be in the bend of your baby's knees and their knees should be slightly above their bottom. You can also lean forward a little while supporting your baby with one arm and use the other arm to reach down and pull the wrap up more to get a better seat for your baby.

Step 3: Next, you'll tighten the wrap. Make sure that you are continuously supporting your baby while you tighten the wrap. Take a hold of the top rail of the wrap on one side and pull it tight. Pulling out and up can help get it as snug as possible. Do this repetitively as you move your grip incrementally towards the bottom rail. Make sure you tighten each part of the wrap. Hold the tail snugly while you repeat this with the other side.

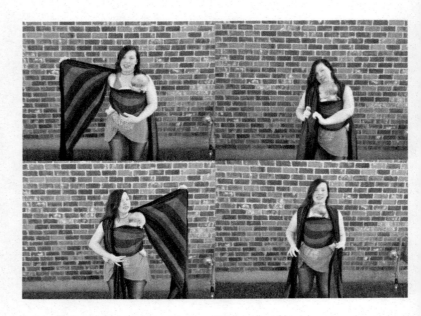

Step 4: Keep both tails snug with one in each hand. Cross the tails underneath your baby's bottom. Then pull them underneath your baby's legs towards your back. Once you have the tails behind you, tie them in a knot. For extra comfort, you can spread the rails across your back and on your shoulders. Make sure your baby's knees are able to easily bend as well.

Rucksack Carry

A rucksack carry, often just called a ruck, is probably the easiest back carry in a woven wrap. It's often the first back carry that someone will learn. It is important that you do not try back carries if you aren't accustomed to using a woven wrap. Ideally, you should be proficient at doing at least a few different front carries before attempting a back carry. You should also start by practicing over a bed or a couch just to be on the safe side.

Step 1: The first step of any back carry is to get your child on your back. There are several different ways you can do this. You can start your child out on your hip and scoot them onto your back, you can lift them over your head and lower them onto your back, or you can toss them onto your back similarly to how you might put on a jacket. The last method is often called the "Superman toss" and is demonstrated in the pictures below. I, personally, find it to be the easiest way to get your child into the best position.

First, you'll place the middle marker of the wrap at the center of your child's back up at the base of their neck. With the wrap going over their shoulders, take a hold of them at their shoulders, under their arms. Get a good grip on them and swing them up and around so that they land at the center of your back up at your shoulders like in the pictures. You'll need to bend over to hold them on your back while you wrap them.

Step 2: Remain bending forward until you secure your child onto your back. You will also want to keep a hand on them at all points until they are secured. Pull both tails forward so they are coming over your

shoulders. You'll need to secure the top rail well while you make a seat for your child in the wrap. You can do this by twisting the top rail of each side together and then pinning it underneath your chin while you make the seat.

Once you've secured the top rail, reach behind you and underneath your child's legs. Grab a hold of the bottom rail of the wrap below your child and pull it up between the two of you. This should pull your child's knees up above their bottom. Then, just like the FWCC, tighten each tail incrementally until the entire wrap is tightened on both sides.

Step 3: Once you have fully tightened each tail, take them in your hands and pull them back behind you above your child's legs. Then cross the tails under your child's bottom and pull them back to your front going under your child's legs this time.

Step 4: Now that you have the tails in front of you, you can tie them at your waist in a double knot. This is the most basic way to finish a ruck, but there are lots of different ways you can tie your tails to create pretty finishes.

Chapter 6: Co-Sleeping: Why Crunchy Parents Sleep Better

Many people don't realize that almost all parents co-sleep with their babies at some point or another. That is because many people think that to co-sleep, you must share the bed with your baby. However, co-sleeping is any time that you share a room with your baby. Since most parents have their newborns start out in their room, even on a different sleeping surface, most parents co-sleep.

When you actually have your baby in your bed with you, it is called bed sharing which is a specific type of co-sleeping. It is a very natural and crunchy practice to bed share with your baby. In fact, many are surprised to learn that much of the world bed shares and America actually has some of the lowest rates of bed sharing.

When my son was born, we didn't plan on bed sharing. However, after several weeks of having him in the bassinet next to our bed, and having to get up a million times a night to nurse him and then put him back to sleep, and feeling like I was just constantly drained and never sleeping myself, we decided to keep him in bed with us. Everything got so much better after that! Then when my daughter was born, we just started keeping her in bed with us right away. I sleep curled around my daughter with the wall on the other side of her. Then my husband and my son sleep behind me however they feel like on any particular night. It works amazingly well for us. All of us, including my husband, love sharing a bed.

Benefits Crunchy Parents Get from Co-Sleeping

There are many wonderful and valuable benefits to be gained from co-sleeping with your baby. There are different ways to co-sleep with your baby including simply having your baby's crib or bassinet in the same room that you sleep in, using a co-sleeper to connect your baby's sleep surface to your bed, or actually sharing the bed with your baby. All forms of co-sleeping provide benefits to you and your baby, but bed sharing with your baby is the best way to receive the maximum benefits of co-sleeping.

Co-Sleeping Babies Wake Less Often

This applies especially to bed sharing, but it can be true of other types of co-sleeping as well. When your baby is in bed with you (or close by), they feel much more secure and safe. They are less likely to wake as often when they're feeling this way. One of the things that may cause your baby to wake in the night is simply because they need physical contact with you, but if they already have that by sharing your bed, they won't be disturbed by that need.

The biggest reasons babies wake in the night is to eat. Babies need to eat often as they have such small stomachs that empty quickly. Bed sharing allows breastfeeding mothers to easily feed their babies in the night without having to get out of bed or move their baby. Often times, the mother is able to feed their baby without the baby ever fully waking. The mother is often able to also sleep in a side-lying nursing position, maximizing sleep for the entire family.

Co-Sleeping Gives You Peace of Mind

It is unnatural to have your baby sleep away from you. If you don't have your baby close by, you will likely have increased anxiety and worry. This can make you feel more restless. Having your baby close by or especially having your baby in bed with you allows you to know that your baby is perfectly okay and safe and that all of their needs are met.

Even the AAP states that there is a reduced risk of SIDS for babies that sleep in the same room as their parents. In addition to the lower risk of SIDS, having your baby close by can help prevent other possible issues such as choking or suffocation. The reason is that you are much more likely to notice that something is wrong before it is too late if you have your baby with you.

Co-Sleeping Increases Bond and Attachment

By sleeping with your baby, you are able to spend more quality time with your baby, you can meet their needs much more quickly, and you are more easily able to develop a strong bond with your baby. This helps to increase the trust and confidence of your baby. Research clearly shows that babies that form strong attachments with caregivers at a young age grow to be more independent and much better-adjusted adults.

Co-Sleeping Safety That Crunchy Parents Need to Know

Co-sleeping, specifically bed sharing, gets a bad reputation for being dangerous. However, there are just a few simple rules to follow that will make bed sharing completely safe. As long as you follow these safe sleeping guidelines, you have no reason to worry about your baby's safety when sharing the bed with them.

No Smoking, Drinking, or Drugs

If you look at cases where infants die in bed with adults, you will find that a reoccurring truth is that in the majority of cases, the adults had been drinking or doing drugs, either prescription or otherwise. This is never safe when sharing the bed with your baby. You should never drink before sleeping with your baby and you should never take any types of drugs that could impair you in any way, even if they are prescribed.

You shouldn't even take drugs that can make you drowsy before sharing the bed with your baby, such as certain allergy medications, because they can cause you to fall into an unnaturally deep sleep which is not safe for your baby. If you must take any type of medication that could make bed sharing unsafe, consider keeping your baby close on a separate sleep surface such as a bassinet or co-sleeper instead of in the bed with you.

Additionally, anyone that smokes cigarettes should not share a bed with a baby. Cigarette smoke is highly toxic and even if you don't smoke around your baby, they can still come in contact with it from your clothes, hair, skin, and mouth. A baby that is exposed to cigarette smoke has a higher risk of SIDS and sleeping with an adult that smokes exposes the baby to the smoke leftover on the adult's skin, clothing, hair or breath for extended periods of time while the baby is sleeping.

Sleep on a Safe Surface

Another very important aspect of safe co-sleeping is making sure that the surface your baby sleeps on is safe for them. There are several things you'll need to ensure to make a safe sleeping surface for your baby. The first thing is to make sure that the sleeping surface is nice and firm. If it is too soft, it can make it hard for your baby to move and they can become trapped with their face in a position where they can suffocate. The same thing can happen on couches or chairs so you should never sleep with your baby on these things.

You'll also want to make sure that there are no hazards on or around your baby's sleeping surface. This can be obvious things like cords or strings but also things like excess bedding. You never want to have a pillow or blanket too close to your baby and it is also a good idea to keep toys away from the sleep surface. You don't want anything around your baby that could pose a suffocation or strangulation risk. You should also keep your baby on their back, or in the case of night nursing, on their side. This will help prevent suffocation and it is also shown to reduce the risk of SIDS.

It is definitely fine for you, and your partner if applicable, to each have a pillow. Just don't have any additional pillows on the bed. It is also okay for you to use a blanket, just keep it low away from your little one. Also keep in mind that you should not swaddle your baby while they share a bed with you. It can cause them to overheat and not be able to move around adequately. If the temperature calls for it, you may use a small, light blanket for your baby but keep it down away from their face and avoid it if possible. Most of the time, your body heat should be plenty enough to keep your baby at a comfortable temperature.

Bed Sharing is Safest When Baby is Breastfed

Bed sharing is safer for your baby if you are breastfeeding your little one full time. That means both day and night. If you are formula feeding or supplementing, there is a chance that bed sharing could pose some risk, so it may be better to consider co-sleeping by having your baby on a separate surface close by if that is the case.

There are a few things that make it safer for breastfed babies to bed share with their parents. One of those things is that breastfed babies arouse more easily which definitely makes bed sharing much safer. Another important reason that it is safer for breastfed babies to bed share is that a breastfeeding mother is very in tune with her baby and therefore much more likely to wake up if there is any danger.

Additionally, a breastfeeding mother instinctively sleeps in the perfect position to keep her baby safe. That is on her side with her baby at breast level and with her knees up and arm out to create a sort of box around the baby. This would prevent another parent from rolling into or onto the baby without waking the mother. For this reason, a baby under the age of 12 months should always sleep next to their mother when bed sharing.

It is also very important to remember that a baby under 12 months of age should never sleep next to an older sibling or other child. Ideally, a child under a year old should be sleeping between their mother and a wall. You don't want to have your baby in a position where they can roll off the bed. If you do need to place your baby between yourself and the edge of the bed, it is a good idea to use a bed rail. You can also have your mattress placed directly on the floor for an added safety measure.

Crunchy Parents Know to Ignore the Myths of Co-Sleeping

Unfortunately, there are plenty of negative myths surrounding co-sleeping. This is likely because it is common to hear of bad experiences with bed sharing with a baby, but of course, you are never going to hear about when it goes well because it is uneventful and is not newsworthy.

"Bed Sharing is Dangerous"

The biggest myth about co-sleeping is that bed sharing is inherently dangerous. This myth no doubt comes from stories of things going wrong because parents or care givers weren't following good safety guidelines when sleeping with their babies. Many of these incidents occur when parents sleep on a couch with their baby, and many others occur when the parent is somehow intoxicated. As long as you follow all of the important safety guidelines with bed sharing, it is completely safe for your little one.

"Your Baby Will Never Sleep on Their Own"

Another common concern people have about co-sleeping is that the child will never learn to sleep on their own. This is, obviously, not true. Babies and young children require lots of love and comfort so it makes complete sense that they sleep with or near their parents. Even many parents that don't choose to co-sleep find that they do end up having their children come into their rooms sometimes. This is completely normal and natural. Every child will, at some point, be ready to sleep on their own.

"You're Preventing Your Child from Learning Independence"

There is nothing independent about a baby. They are, in their very nature, completely dependent beings. There is nothing wrong with this and there is especially nothing wrong with catering to their needs. One of those very important needs is love, closeness, and attachment to a parent or caregiver. Co-sleeping helps to provide for those needs and in no way harms your baby eventually learning independence. In fact, co-sleeping helps to foster a strong parent-child bond and gives the child confidence they need to become very independent as they grow.

Chapter 7: Crunchy Parents Believe in Bodily Autonomy

Bodily autonomy is the concept that a person has the right to have complete control over their body and what happens to or with their body. They make all decisions regarding their body. It simply is not right to force a person to do anything with their body, including forcing them to alter their body in any way, without their informed consent. The majority of crunchy parents believe very strongly in the importance of bodily autonomy for everyone, including children.

Their Body, Their Choice

There are some situations where parents violate their child's right to bodily autonomy by making unnecessary and often harmful decisions regarding the child's body. Most of the time, these violations of bodily autonomy come from cultural or religious traditions. These harmful traditions negatively impact children all around the world in different ways.

Some areas and cultures practice something called scarification where they force a child to endure them cutting into their skin, often on the face, to create scars. These scars are often status symbols of some kind and are usually considered beautiful by the people in that culture. The children who were cut grow up and continue the cycle of cutting children because it is what they are used to and they feel that it is normal and acceptable.

Other areas and cultures practice body modifications of different types on their infants or children. Some examples include stretching the skin of the ears or lips, piercing or tattooing various parts of the body, using coils around the neck to lower the shoulders and give the neck an elongated appearance, and the infamous female genital mutilation (FGM), also known as female circumcision.

There are two main ways that our culture violates the bodily autonomy of our children, and chances are that you think of these things as normal and acceptable if you were raised in this society. Those things are piercing the ears of babies and male infant circumcision. These things are often defended as parental choices, but if you open your mind, take time to educate yourself, and just think about it logically, you will realize that these choices do not belong to the parents, but to the person whose body is affected by the choice.

The child is the one that not only has to endure the body modification, but has to live with it for the rest of their lives. It affects the child, not the parents, therefore it should be the child's choice. Ear piercings can be taken out without causing too much long-lasting damage, but it should still be the child's choice if they want a piercing or not. Just imagine if you found out that your neighbor had their daughter's belly button, eyebrow, or nose pierced. They could easily use all the same arguments to defend it as someone would defend ear piercing. The only difference is that one is accepted by our society and the others are not.

Male infant circumcision is much more damaging and permanent than ear piercing, but is still found as acceptable by our society. A baby that is circumcised has an important and functioning body part amputated from them typically when they are just a few days or sometimes only a few hours old. They never have a choice in how much of their body that they get to keep and they can never reverse the decision that was made for them. However, if they are left intact, they can make the decision themselves when they are of age and able to understand all of the possible consequences.

Drawbacks of Circumcision that Crunchy Parents Avoid

The majority of people in our society believe that circumcision is beneficial in several ways, and are surprised to find out that actually the opposite is true and circumcision is actually very harmful and has no real benefits. Understanding the history of circumcision can help you to better understand the drawbacks of circumcision.

Circumcision used to be only performed as a religious ceremony, but in the late 1800s/early 1900s, a doctor named John Harvey Kellogg began to promote circumcision as a way to prevent masturbation in males. He also used pure carbolic acid on the clitoris of females to prevent female masturbation.

Luckily, that one didn't catch on. Unfortunately, male circumcision did. Obviously, it did not serve its intended purpose of preventing masturbation, but the practice of routine infant circumcision was developed and continued because of the supposed health benefits that circumcision held.

You've probably heard things like circumcision reduces the chance of STDs, penile cancer, and UTIs, but as it turns out most of the supposed benefits of circumcision don't exist at all. Studies do show that there is a reduced risk of these things, but the reduction in risk shown is extremely minor and the studies are very flawed anyways.

What you probably have not heard is about the risks involved and drawbacks of circumcision and that is probably not by accident or coincidence. The vast majority of the world understands how important the foreskin is and how ridiculous it is to cut it off of babies but for some reason, America doesn't seem to get it. It might just have to do with the fact that circumcision is a multi-million-dollar industry.

There is actually a group of doctors that have formed an organization called Doctors Opposing Circumcision that advocates against the practice of circumcision on babies. These are ethical doctors that have done their research and understand how harmful it really is. They gain nothing other than knowing they are spreading knowledge by participating in the organization. So, who are you going to believe? The doctor that will make hundreds of dollars off of a 20-minute procedure if you choose to do it, or the doctors that have dedicated their time and energy to educating you about why you shouldn't do it?

Circumcision Causes Trauma

When a boy is born, his foreskin is fused to the glans to protect it. Usually sometime between the age of 3 and puberty, the foreskin will naturally start to retract. The foreskin still remains over the glans most of the time, unless the penis is erect. The fusion between the foreskin and the glans must be broken for amputation to occur. So, the first step of circumcision is to rip the foreskin away from the glans. This alone is painful, but it is only the first step and not the worst by far.

Once the foreskin is ripped from the glans, one of several methods is used to clamp and cut the foreskin off. In other words, an infant circumcision consists of the baby's penis being ripped, crushed, and cut. There is one method of circumcision that is advertised as less painful because it doesn't involve cutting called the Plastibel method.

However, it actually does involve a small amount of cutting before closing a piece of plastic around the foreskin. This crushes the foreskin, cutting off blood supply. The result is that the tissue dies and falls off. That wouldn't exactly be less painful. This is all happening to an hours-old to days-old infant.

Even worse is that an infant this age cannot safely receive the anaesthesia that would be required to combat the pain involved. For this reason, they either receive only a local pain reliever that proves ineffective, or in many cases, they receive no pain medication at all.

More often than not, a baby's reaction to such severe pain and trauma is to shut down completely. Babies often pass out due to shock, but parents are usually told that their baby is just sleeping. Circumcision can have a severe negative impact on bonding and breastfeeding with your new baby as well.

Circumcision Carries Serious Risks

Since there are no real benefits to circumcision, it is now largely considered to be a cosmetic procedure. It is truly unethical to perform a medically unnecessary cosmetic procedure on a newborn baby, but it is still done and like all surgeries, it carries some serious risks. The fact that surgery is being carried out on a highly vascular area on a newborn makes the surgery even riskier.

For example, a newborn baby only has a very small amount of blood in their body. For this reason, it only takes just over 2 ounces of blood loss for a baby to die from blood loss. This alone is reason enough to not perform circumcision on babies, but there are many other risks involved as well. Circumcision can lead to painful adhesions, buried penis syndrome, phimosis, painful erections, severe scarring, erectile dysfunction, and other problems and complications as well.

Circumcision Causes the Loss of Important Functions

In our pro-circumcision society, the foreskin is often referred to as a useless little flap of skin, but how much do you actually know about the foreskin? An adult male loses about 15 square inches of skin to circumcision. That seems like more than just a little flap. As it turns out, the foreskin actually serves several very important purposes as well.

One very important thing that the male foreskin, also known as the prepuce, does is protect the glans (head) of the penis. In an intact male, the glans is soft, smooth, and moist. It is more similar to the inside of a woman's vagina and is designed to be a primarily internal organ. Circumcision causes the glans to be continually exposed which over time causes it to become rough, dry, and calloused.

The foreskin also contains a massive amount of nerve endings that are designed to increase pleasure during sex. It also provides lubrication for sex. As it turns out, contrary to popular belief, the woman is not the only one that is supposed to provide lubrication for sex. In addition to providing extra lubrication, the foreskin provides protection against painful friction during intercourse. It is important to research the functions of the foreskin that are lost due to circumcision so that you can make a fully educated decision about it.

Cognitive Dissonance

Cognitive dissonance is likely one of the number one reasons that the cycle of male circumcision continues. Cognitive dissonance is a term used to describe the uncomfortable conflict that occurs in the brain when new information contradicts previously held beliefs. This is why it is so hard to change someone's mind once it is made up. The person can't deal with the conflict so they either must let go of their belief and admit that they were wrong or they must deny and not accept the new information.

Many people in our society struggle with this because admitting that they were wrong to think circumcision is wrong is a very personal thing for them. This is either because they were circumcised themselves, or because they chose to have their child circumcised. So rather than admit that they are missing something or that they took something away from their child, they continue to defend circumcision even when facts prove that it is dangerous, harmful and unethical. This all happens in a person's subconscious, so they truly believe that they are right.

Proper Intact Care for Crunchy Parents and Their Sons

Another one of the myths of circumcision is that intact penises are hard to properly care for. Many parents are given improper instructions on how to clean their son's intact penis which can lead to problems. In fact, the problems associated with improper care of the intact penis are actually the biggest source of the myths of problems related to being intact, such as a higher rate of infections.

It turns out that care of an intact penis is very simple. When cared for properly, problems of the intact penis are uncommon. Since the foreskin is fused to the glans of the penis at birth, the foreskin should never be forcibly retracted. Retracting the foreskin before it starts to naturally retract on its own can be painful and damaging.

Instead, all you have to do at diaper changes is simply wipe the penis from base to tip as you would a finger. There is no reason to try to clean inside the foreskin and trying to do so could cause infection and other harm to your baby. As your son grows older, his foreskin will eventually begin to retract on its own and at that point, he should be the only one to ever retract it for any reason.

Chapter 8: Crunchy Parents Choose Natural Immunity

The human body is an amazing thing and is designed exceptionally well. It has a plethora of different ways that it impressively functions. We have learned so much about the way our bodies work, yet we have so much left still to learn. One fascinating thing about our body is the way that so many of our body parts all work together to protect us from outside harm such as viruses and diseases. This defense network is known as our immune system.

Crunchy Parents Understand the Dangers of Vaccinating

Vaccines are substances that are introduced to the body, usually by injection, in order to create an artificial immunity to a specific disease. The substance contains either a dead or living virus or bacterium which is what solicits the response from the immune system. The first vaccine was created in the late 1700s and tons more have been created since and more are still being created today.

In fact, the number of recommended vaccines during childhood has grown significantly. A child that is vaccinated according to the current schedule that the CDC recommends will receive close to 40 different shots throughout childhood. Close to 30 of those occur in the first 18 months of the child's life with multiple shots each containing multiple vaccines being administrated at the same time.

Vaccines carry many risks and there is a long and scary list of problems ranging from minor irritation all the way to death that can occur as a result of vaccines. It isn't just speculation or conspiracy theories either, even the vaccine manufacturers themselves admit that the vaccines can cause a range of serious complications including death. Anybody can request an insert from the vaccines that their child is supposed to receive at the pediatrician where you can read about some of the dangers, risks, as well as the ingredients of the vaccine, or you can find these things on the CDC website.

When you learn about the ingredients that are in vaccines, you may be shocked. This substance that you are supposed to allow someone to inject into your child's body contains many dangerous, toxic, and some just flat out disturbing ingredients. Many vaccines contain heavy metals, formaldehyde, tissue from the hearts of cows, protein from chicken eggs, and even tissue from aborted human babies. That is only just scratching the surface of the ingredients used in vaccines.

Interestingly enough, the manufacturers of vaccines hold absolutely no liability for any problems caused by vaccines. Legally, they cannot be touched, even if a vaccine that they created causes death. Instead, the government has several things in place for people that have problems arise after receiving vaccines. VAERS is the shortened name of the Vaccine Adverse Events Reporting System where consumers are able to submit reports of adverse events occurring after vaccination. The government also has a program called the Vaccine Injury Compensation Program (VICP) and has paid out nearly $4 billion to vaccine-injured people and their families since it was established in 1986.

Problems with the Pro-Vax Argument

Supporters of vaccination often use flawed logic and fear mongering as ways to try to convince others that they must vaccinate their children. It is not uncommon for those that are pro-vaccination to attempt to belittle anyone who suggests that it may not be the best choice to vaccinate and they often act as though anyone who questions vaccination is idiotic. That in and of itself is a serious problem. As parents, we should always question everything when it comes to our kids. If something can't stand up to that questioning, then obviously it is not the best choice for our kids.

Herd Immunity is a Lie

One of the most common things that tends to come up in the pro-vax argument is how important herd immunity is. Herd immunity is the concept that if the vast majority of the population is vaccinated, that it will protect the entire population, including those that are too young or unwell to receive vaccinations because the diseases in question are unable to spread through the vaccinated "herd".

The biggest problem with the herd immunity argument is that many adults do not stay up-to-date with their vaccinations past childhood. That means that a large chunk of the population is not vaccinated at all which means that herd immunity would be ineffective anyways whether or not all children are vaccinated.

Unvaccinated Children Do Not Pose a Risk

Another one of the biggest arguments that some people use when trying to convince others to vaccinate is that unvaccinated children are dangerous and will spread diseases to other children. This notion is ridiculous for a few reasons. First of all, a healthy unvaccinated child cannot spread a disease that they don't even have.

Also, if the people who are so worried about that have vaccinated their child, why would they be worried about their child getting a disease they have been vaccinated against if the vaccine is supposed to be effective? Then that leads to another flaw in the argument because vaccines are not always effective. Some vaccines are not effective at all, but none even claim to be completely effective.

As in, vaccinated kids can get and spread these diseases anyways. Finally, some people say that unvaccinated children pose a risk to babies and children that are too young to be vaccinated as well as unwell people that are immunocompromised such as a chemo patient. The problem here is that unless the unvaccinated child has actually come in contact with and contracted the disease, they obviously can't spread it.

However, vaccinated children have come in direct contact with the diseases through the vaccines. In fact, it is recommended to keep immunocompromised people away from children that have recently been vaccinated because some vaccines can actually shed and spread the disease to others, especially babies and immunocompromised people.

You Are Not Putting Your Child in Danger by Not Vaccinating

One more claim that pro-vaxxers use is that by not vaccinating your child, you are putting them in serious danger. They believe that if you don't vaccinate your child that they are likely to contract a deadly disease. This really isn't the case, though. Sure, some vaccines may reduce your chance of getting certain diseases, but what many people seem to not realize is that most things that we vaccinate against are not that big of a deal.

This is especially true now with modern medicine. Most things that are vaccinated against pose no serious risk if the child contracts the disease. In fact, most things that are vaccinated against resolve on their own. Besides, vaccinated children can still get the diseases they are vaccinated against so by vaccinating, you are not only putting your child at risk of all the potential side effects of vaccines including death, but they still might get the diseases anyways.

Crunchier Ways to Boost Immunity

The human immune system is designed very well and is usually very effective in protecting us from outside dangers. Even when we do come down with some kind of illness, our immune system quickly learns and will protect us from the same thing in the future. There are some great ways that we can support our immune system and keep it nice and healthy so that it can keep us nice and healthy as well.

Breastfeeding

The first and probably the best way that you can give your child's immune system a natural and very effective boost is by breastfeeding. Breastmilk contains tons of antibodies and helps boost the immune system of your little one as well as helps it to develop properly. Your child's immune system is not fully developed until around 7 or so years of age so breastfeeding can make a major difference in how efficiently your child's immune system fights off outside dangers.

Diet

Beyond just breastfeeding, the other things that your child consumes are important as well when it comes to keeping them as healthy as possible. All of the different parts of your body work better and more efficiently when you have a healthy and proper diet. Try to make sure your child gets a good variety of healthy food options to help ensure they get adequate amounts of all important vitamins, minerals, and other nutrients. It is also an excellent idea to eat clean by choosing non-GMO and organic options to help avoid dangerous toxins like pesticides, unnatural hormones, and antibiotics.

Environmental Factors

It is not just what we put into our bodies that can make a difference in how our bodies and immune systems work. The other products that we use daily can make a big difference too. It is best to avoid toxins of all kinds inside and outside of the body. Choose more natural options for cleaning both your body, your child's body, and your home in order to avoid harsh and dangerous chemicals and other ingredients which can negatively impact your child's body and how efficiently things like their immune system may work.

Conclusion: Crunchy Parenting is Natural and Easy

Overall, crunchy parenting is very simple and easy. The main concept behind parenting crunchy is about a solid mixture of parenting by both instincts and in an evidence-based way. It may seem difficult at first, but many aspects of crunchy parenting are actually much easier than mainstream methods when it comes down to it and are definitely worth your efforts. Crunchy parenting may be seen as weird or bizarre in our mainstream society, but it is gaining popularity as more people learn the facts and it really is a more natural approach to raising kids that has many amazing benefits for both you and your children.

About the Expert

Madi Haire is the mother of two amazing children – Adam and Zelda. She gave birth to both of them naturally without pain medication and have experience with tandem-breastfeeding. She and her husband both work from home so that they can all stay together as much as possible. Through in-depth research, they have found that the best parenting choices tend to be the more natural and crunchy ones. Some of their crunchy parenting choices (that are all completely backed up by research) include breastfeeding, co-sleeping, respecting their children's rights to bodily autonomy, and babywearing. Haire is also the leader in her local babywearing group and always aims to help provide gentle education to parents in order to help them make well-informed, evidence-based, and natural decisions.

HowExpert publishes short 'how to' guides on unique topics by everyday experts.

Recommended Resources

www.HowExpert.com – Short 'how to' guides on unique topics by everyday experts!

www.HowExpert.com/parenting - Additional resource related to parenting tips!

Lightning Source UK Ltd.
Milton Keynes UK
UKOW04f1129020118
315271UK00005B/214/P